24 Games You Can Play on a
CHECKER BOARD

Carol Lynch Williams

Illustrations by Jennifer Kalis

Gibbs Smith, Publisher
TO ENRICH AND INSPIRE HUMANKIND
Salt Lake City | Charleston | Santa Fe | Santa Barbara

To Laura Torres
my friend across the miles

First Edition
11 10 09 08 07   5 4 3 2 1

Text © 2007 Carol Lynch Williams
Illustrations © 2007 Jennifer Kalis
Designs © 2007 Dawn DeVries Sokol

Published by
Gibbs Smith, Publisher
P.O. Box 667
Layton, Utah 84041

Orders: 1.800.835.4993
www.gibbs-smith.com

Designed by Dawn DeVries Sokol
Printed and bound in China

Library of Congress Cataloging-in-Publication Data
Williams, Carol Lynch.
24 games you can play on a checkerboard / by Carol Lynch Williams ; illustrations by Jennifer Kalis. — 1st ed.
    p. cm.
  ISBN-10: 1-4236-0011-8
  ISBN-13: 978-1-4236-0011-4
  1. Board games—Juvenile literature. I. Kalis, Jennifer, ill. II. Title. III. Title: Twenty-four games you can play on a checkerboard.

GV1312.W55 2008
794—dc22
                        2006023184

CONTENTS

The Games We Can Play

CHECKERS HAS BEEN AROUND FOR AGES.
And I mean AGES. Sure, people played the game in England
(it's called Draughts there) for several hundred years. And it's
been played in America for a long time, too. But get this:
People in Egypt around 1600 BC were playing a game that
may have been similar to what we call Checkers today. It's
cool to think about the game being that old.

This book has **24 different games you can play on a
checkerboard** (including the directions to a plain ol' game of
checkers). Some are pretty easy to learn. **Most make you
really think.** On some you'll want to plan a strategy—just
like in regular checkers or chess. Read through all the instruc-
tions a couple of times before you begin to play a new game.

So find a friend and get playing. While no game in this
collection is as old as the ones in Egyptian paintings,
**you can bet you're going to
have fun.**

4

On some of these games you can only play in certain squares on the board. For more complicated game setups, you may want to lightly trace the playing area onto the board using a pencil or a dry-erase marker that can be wiped clean after you finish your game.

Name of the Game:
Traditional Checkers

Here are the rules to playing a simple game of checkers. Once you learn these, you should be able to master any game in this book. So get ready to have some fun!

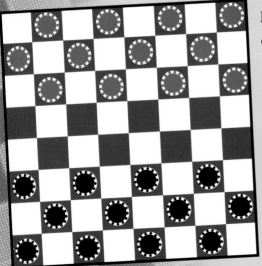

Each player gets 12 pieces, red for one person, black for the other.

You'll play only on the black squares. Starting on the back line, fill in each black square on the first three lines with your checker pieces, as shown in the diagram.

Flip a coin for your game piece color. Black moves first.

Your Move

You'll move only one
space at a time and
always on the diagonal.

You can only move in
the forward direction.

3 You can only jump
a checker if the player is in the adjacent, diagonal
position to your checker. There must also be an
empty square for your playing piece to land on.

When you jump an opponent's
playing piece, you capture it and
remove it from the board.

5 You must jump if there's an opening. And you must jump all pieces that are available to jump on that turn.

6 Work to get your playing pieces onto the back line of squares on your opponent's side of the board. When you get a checker piece there, your piece gets "crowned" and becomes a King. Crown your piece by turning it over to show the crown or by placing a second checker on top of it.

7 A King can move in any direction—forward or backward—but the moves must be diagonal.

The Goal

You want to capture, or jump, all your opponent's pieces.

And the winner is! The person who either can keep his or her opponent from moving, or who captures all of the opponent's playing pieces.

Name of the Game:
The Coyote
AND THE CHICKENS

If you're playing this game, you may get hungry (hey, there are chickens involved here). Whatever you do, don't eat the playing pieces!

You'll need 12 game pieces of one color to be the Chickens, and 1 game piece of another color to be the Coyote.

You'll play on the black squares of the board. The Chickens fill up the first three rows of black squares. The Coyote takes position on the opposite side of the board, in the corner on the black square. See the diagram.

The Chickens start the game (see, they're not *that* chicken).

Your Move

1 The Chickens can only move one space at a time, staying on the black squares and moving diagonally.

2 They can only go forward, never backward. They cannot jump.

3 The lone Coyote has all the power, though he is out-numbered. He can move forward and backward (diagonally only, staying on the black).

4 He can only move one space at a time. The Coyote can also jump and capture the Chickens, removing them from the board. He can do multiple jumps when possible.

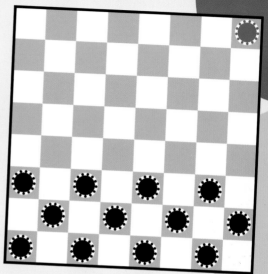

The Goal

The Chickens must corner the Coyote so he can no longer move. The goal for the Coyote is to get to the black corner of the board opposite from where he started. He can jump the Chickens, capturing them until none remain, or he can outmaneuver them, leading them on a wild chicken chase.

And the winner is! Whoever reaches his or her goal wins the game.

Name of the Game:
Alquerque

Each player gets 12 game pieces, red for one person and black for the other.

Setup is as follows:

- Place 5 pieces on the intersections of the back line.

- Place 5 pieces on the intersections of the second line.

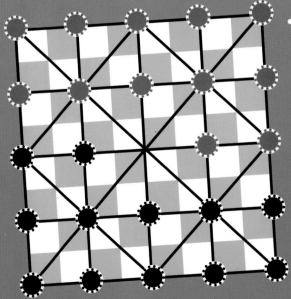

- Place 2 pieces—from your left—on the third line.

Decide who goes first. Toss a coin, or just be generous and let the other player start.

Your Move

1 You move on the lines forward, backward, vertically, horizontally, or diagonally.

2 You capture a checker by jumping it.

3 Multiple jumps are allowed. You have to jump if you can. You can't opt out. If you make a mistake and don't jump a piece, your opponent can take your playing piece.

The Goal

Conquer the world! (Or at least the checkerboard.) Capture all your enemy's playing pieces.

And the winner is! The winner is the person who gets all the opponent's pieces. If neither of you captures all the other person's pieces, the game is a draw (nobody wins).

Name of the Game:

Achi

If you don't feel like playing this game in the house, you could go outside and play in the dirt. Draw a game board with your finger or a stick and use stones as markers.

Each player gets 3 playing pieces.

There is no setup. You take turns placing checkers on the board. Decide who goes first.

FORWARD

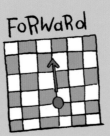

HORIZONTALLY

BACKWARD

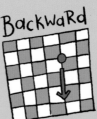

DiagoNALL

Your Move

Take turns placing pieces on the intersections. Think ahead. Can you get 3 in a row with your first strategic move?

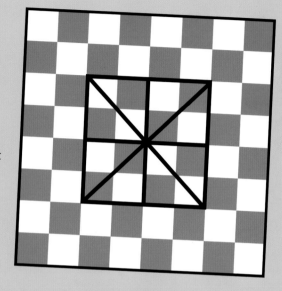

The Goal

You want to line up 3 checkers in a row vertically, horizontally, or diagonally. Keep your checkers on the bold lines. See diagram.

And the winner is! If no one wins immediately, well, the game is not over. Just keep trying. Move one piece at a time until someone gets 3 in a row. What? You're still at it? I'm going to bed.

Name of the Game:
Pyramid CHECKERS

Thank goodness you don't have to work in the hot sun building pyramids. Instead, you can just play this game.

You'll play the black squares of the board.

Each player gets 10 playing pieces.

Set up as follows: Put your playing pieces on the board in the shape of a triangle, as shown in the diagram. Here's how you do it.

- Start with the first row closest to the bottom of the board.

- Put down 4 playing pieces on the black squares.

- For the second row, start at the left, and place 3 playing pieces on the three black squares.

- The third row will take 2.

- The last row will take 1. Wasn't that a lot easier than what the Egyptians went through?

■ Your opponent should set up the same as you did. If not, the game won't work.

▨ Every row has a playing piece when the game begins. If you need help, ask your "mummy."

Decide who starts the game.

Your Move

1 You each can move only one piece at a time, forward only.

2 Your moves must be on the diagonal. Stay on the black!

3 You can jump a piece as in regular checkers, but you do not capture your opponent's piece with this move. It just gets you closer to your goal.

 4 You cannot jump over your own pieces.

 5 If neither of you can make a move, the game is a draw.

The Goal The goal is for you to get all of your playing pieces to where your opponent's pyramid was, first. The two of you are trading places.

And the winner is! You become Pharaoh when you've built your pyramid on the opposite side of the board in your opponent's place. Congratulations!

Name of the Game:

Box the Fox

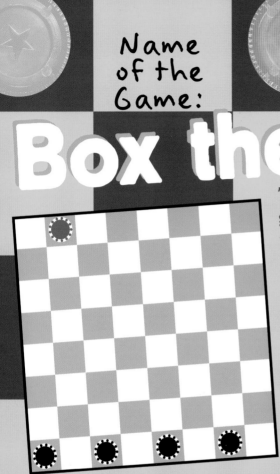

This is a hunting game. But the prey is just the checkers.

You'll play on the black squares on the board. Whoever is the Geese gets 4 playing pieces of one color. The Fox-y player gets 1 piece of a different color.

Line up the Geese on one side of the board, in the last row closest to the back edge. Remember to stay on the black squares. The Fox can choose where he wants to start on the opposite side of the board, in the back row. Black only for him, too.

The Geese start the game, moving just one piece.

Your Move

1 Geese can move forward, just one square at a time. They can go diagonally, either to the right or the left.

2 The Fox is even luckier. He can move any way, diagonally, forward or backward. But he cannot capture the Geese. That means he will always be up against four Geese checkers.

3 Here's the harder part: the Fox can't jump any Geese. That critter just has to think his way to the far side of the board.

The Goal The Geese want to keep the Fox from getting on their back row. They want to "box the fox" in so he can't move anymore. The goal of the Fox is to get on any black square in the last row on the opposite side of the board.

And the winner is! If the Fox makes it to any black square on the far side of the board—you know, the place where the Geese started?—the Fox is the winner. If the Geese keep him from reaching his destination and box him in so he can't move anymore, they have outfoxed the Fox and they win.

Name of the Game:

Giveaway Checkers
(OR THE LOSING GAME)

This game is for people with a generous heart.

You play on the black squares of the board.

Each player gets 12 checker pieces, one color for each of you.

Arrange the board just as you would if you were playing a standard game of checkers—not this friendly, generous game of Giveaway. Line up your pieces on the first three rows of black squares.

Black begins.

Your Move

Remember, the goal of this game is for you to lose your pieces, not save them as you would in a regular game of checkers.

1 Each player can move in the diagonal, forward direction.

2 Try to get your pieces out there so that they are captured.

3 Intentionally move into the path of your opponent. Think ahead.

4 If you can set it up so that your opponent has to jump you, go for it. The more jumps the better.

5 Whatever you do, try *not* to be crowned. You want to stay away from your opponent's back line.

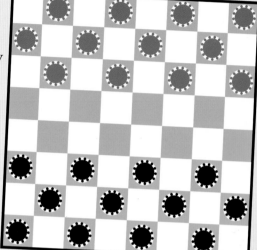

6 Corner yourself, if possible.

The Goal You want to lose—either by having all your pieces captured or by being unable to make any more moves.

And the winner is! The loser!

Name of the Game:
Diagonal Checkers

Okay—turn that board around. More, more, more—there! You got it. When you set up a game of Diagonal Checkers you turn the game board until the white corner points at you. Now you're ready to set up the game.

Each player gets 12 playing pieces, a different color for each person.

With the board turned in this fancy-schmancy direction, start placing your pieces on the black squares. The first row has two spaces, the second has four and the third has six. See the diagram.

Now move the playing board back to its original position.

Black starts the game.

Your Move

1   Check out your opponent's back line. There are only two places for you to go to become King, but that is where you are headed.

2 Move forward on the diagonal to an empty space.

3 Just like in regular checkers, uncrowned pieces can only move forward—even when jumping.

4 The Kings can move forward or backward. That's why they're the Kings. They get to do whatever they want. **Kings Rule!**

The Goal Get to those two back squares and get crowned so you can move all over the place, jumping everyone who comes at you. In the beginning you'll have to jump and be jumped. So think ahead. Your options are limited from the start.

And the winner is! Well, the person who captures all his or her opponent's playing pieces.

Name of the Game:
Dama Checkers
(TURKISH)

Checkers in Turkey is called Dama checkers.

In this game, you and your opponent each get 16 playing pieces instead of 12.

Do you remember that old saying, "Change is good"? Well, not only is it good in Dama, but it is essential. Put your pieces on your second and third rows, as in the diagram. Leave that back row empty. There's more. Place your pieces on all the spaces—both black and white—on your two rows (leaving the row closest to you empty).

Black starts the game.

Your Move

1 Move one space at a time. In this game, you can move *forward* or *sideways*, not diagonally. When you jump your opponent's playing piece, you must jump in the forward or sideways direction, not on the diagonal.

2 You want to get to your opponent's empty back row. Once you do, you are crowned King. You can do this by turning the checker over to show the crown or by stacking a second piece on top of the checker.

3 The King can still move only one space at a time—but now you have more freedom. *Forward* moves, *sideways* moves, and *backward* moves are A-OK once you become King. But you can never move diagonally.

The Goal

Crown as many pieces as you can and wipe out your opponent's pieces by jumping them.

And the winner is! The person with the most playing pieces left, of course.

Name of the Game:

French
Checkers

The hardest part about this game is that you have to play the whole thing while speaking with a French accent and wearing a beret.

You and your opponent each get the regular 12 playing pieces (did you read that direction with an accent?).

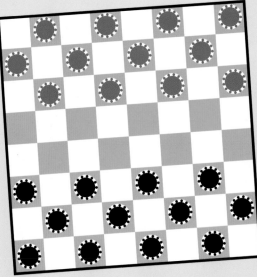

Set up the board in the traditional way. Use the back three rows, putting pieces on the black squares.

Black starts the game.

Your Move

 Uncrowned checkers may move forward in the traditional way, on the diagonal.

 Uncrowned checkers cannot jump forward. In fact, they can only jump *backward*.

3 When a piece has become King then it can jump forward and backward.

The Goal

Mon Ami: Capture the enemy and become King—err Kings.

And the winner is! The person with the most Kings.

Name of the Game:

Checkers
Go-Moku

This is a take on a Japanese game called *Go*. The best way to enjoy this game is with sushi or boiled soybeans.

You and your opponent each get 12 playing pieces, one color for each person.

Black always starts the game.

Your Move

1 In order to capture your opponent's pieces, you have to get 5 of your pieces in a line in adjacent—or touching—squares. This means you have to plan ahead.

2 Black places a piece on any square on the board. It doesn't matter which color of square—choose black or white.

3 The other player puts a checker on the board.

4 Take turns until all 24 pieces are placed.

5 Now—remembering what the goal is—try to keep your pieces as close together as possible.

6 Your opponent will lay pieces in such a way as to get several in a row, too. But you will both try to keep the other person from succeeding.

7 Once all the pieces are down, you will take turns moving your pieces one at a time. You can move in any direction as long as you move to an empty square that is adjacent to the one your checker is on.

8 As you line up your checkers (and block your opponent from doing the same)—work toward getting 5 in a row in any direction.

9 Once you have accomplished this amazing feat, you can remove one of your opponent's playing pieces.

10 Look over the board carefully. You'll want to take a piece from a line that is getting close to 5 checkers in a row. Once you do that, your opponent is going to have to work to get all those checkers back into a 5-piece line.

The Goal You want to capture the other player's pieces.

And the winner is! You win the game when your opponent has only 4 playing pieces left. Why? She doesn't have enough checkers to make a line 5 pieces long.

Name of the Game:

Four-Field
KONO

You're still playing on a checkerboard, but the field is getting a little smaller. In this game you aren't going to trap a piece, or jump over a piece. You are jumping *on* the piece to capture it.

Each player gets 8 playing pieces.

Put your pieces on the corners of the nine boxes as shown in the diagram. You each get two lines.

Check out the diagram on page 35 so you get things set up just right. You might want to sketch in the lines on the board for this game.

Choose who goes first.

Your Move

1 Move by jumping over one of your *own* pieces, along the line of the board.

2 Jump right on top of your opponent's playing piece and take it as your own, removing it from the board.

 3 Leave your piece where your opponent's was.

4 Now your opponent does the same thing.

 5 Go back and forth making captures.

6 When you can no longer jump over your own piece, slide down the line your piece is on until you can move. You don't move on the diagonal in this game; you follow the line that the board makes. And you never move outside of the nine boxes you have created for your playing pieces.

The Goal Capture all your opponent's playing pieces.

And the winner is! Whoever has the most of the other person's playing pieces, wins.

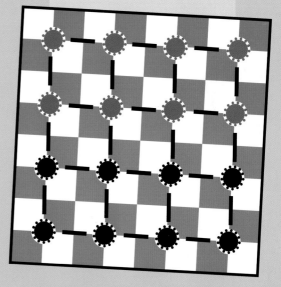

Five-Field Kono

5⁵
5 5

Okay, things might look a little the same as in **Four-Field Kono,** but you play this game differently from the last. At least you know the setup, right?

Place your 7 pieces on the corners of 4 boxes as shown in the diagram. You might want to sketch in the lines on the board for this game.

You decide who goes first.

Your Move

1 Take turns moving diagonally across the squares to the opposite side of the board.

2 Remember to land on *intersections of the black lines* of the playing board.

You can move forward or backward.

 You can't jump your opponent's pieces, and you can't capture them either.

 Make sure you play on the intersections of the lines (rather than on the squares) for this game.

The Goal

Move all your pieces to where your opponent began. That's right. You end up where he started.

And the winner is!

The person who gets over to the other side of the board first.

Name of the Game:
Three Men's
MORRIS

Can you believe that there are so many men named Morris!

Each player gets 3 checkers, one color for each of you.

Take turns putting your checkers on the intersections of the board, one at a time. There are nine possible places you can go, as shown in the diagram. Only move once per turn.

Decide who goes first. If you want to be nice this time, let your opponent have the first move.

Your Move

1   As you place your checker pieces down, try to get 3 in a row.

2 If both players have put all their pieces down and neither one of you have won, play still continues. Remove one of your pieces and see if you can maneuver into a better position.

3 Play continues until one of you succeeds in getting 3 checkers in a row.

4 You can't win with a diagonal set of 3. You have to stay on horizontal or vertical lines.

The Goal It's so easy. You want to get 3 of your pieces in a straight line either vertically or horizontally.

And the winner is! The person who gets 3 pieces in a row wins the game. (I told you this was an easy game.)

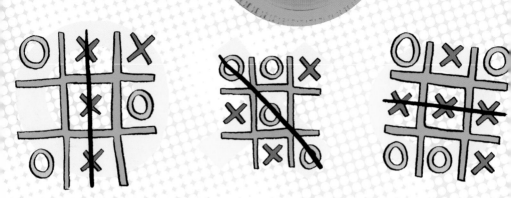

Name of the Game:
Seega

This game is a little like Tic-Tac-Toe.

Each player gets 3 checkers, one color for each of you.

You're playing in nine squares only. Look at the diagram so you see what we mean. Now, put your 3 checkers in the three squares closest to you. Your opponent places her checkers in the three squares closest to her.

Decide who goes first. If you're playing with your mom, say to her, "You go first, Mom. Age before beauty." That should rattle her and give you a bit of an advantage so you can win the game.

Your Move
1
You may move your checkers either one or two spaces at a time.

2 You choose the direction—forward, backward, or diagonal.

3 You can't jump your opponent's checker piece.

4 And you can't have 2 pieces in the same square.

5 You can only move into empty squares, and there are only three of them. So think ahead.

The Goal Simple! Get your 3 pieces in the same row. Again the row can go in any direction—horizontally, vertically or diagonally.

And the winner is! Whoever gets 3 pieces in the same row (but not the same row you started in).

Name of the Game: Wolf

AND GOATS

Here's a game you can play that has one player outnumbered by an opponent. It's a little like Box the Fox.

The Wolf player gets just 1 checker. The Goats player gets 12 checkers.

Goats set up on the black squares of the board, just like if you were playing a regular game of checkers. Fill up all three lines with those 12 checkers, on the black squares only. The Wolf can choose one of two places to go—either the black square on the right or the black square on the left in the back line opposite the Goats.

Toss a coin to see who begins play.

 1 Players always move on the diagonal— and only one square at a time.

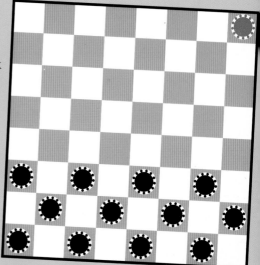

2 The Goats—who want to block the Wolf—can go only in the forward diagonal direction.

3 But the Wolf—lucky dog—can move forward or backward. Remember, he has to go diagonally, too.

4 He can jump the Goats, just like in regular checkers, and remove them from the board.

5 Once the Goats get to the opposite side of the board from where they started, they cannot move.

The Goal The Goats want to keep the Wolf from getting to the far side of the board. The Wolf wants to get at that back line.

And the winner is! Whoever reaches his or her goal first. The Goats win if they stop the Wolf. The Wolf wins if he reaches the back line.

43

Name of the Game:

Lasca

You're gonna be piling checkers pretty high in this game, so you better get a building permit before you start playing!

Each player gets 11 pieces (called Soldiers).

You're playing on a seven by seven board. If you don't set up the board exactly how it is shown in the diagram on page 46, you can't play this game. You might want to sketch in the lines on the board to help you stay in the right place. The regular side of the checker faces up. Fill in the back three rows with your 11 pieces. Play is on the white squares.

Red checkers start the game.

Your Move

1 You are headed to the opposite side of the board. You can only move on the diagonal. And you can jump your opponent just like in regular checkers—in fact, you have to jump. When you make it to your opponent's back line, you flip your checker over and it becomes an Officer. That ol' Officer can move forward and backward, but only on the diagonal. Remember to stay on the white squares.

2 Here's where the game gets really fun. When any playing piece jumps another, you do not remove the piece from the board.

3 Instead, you make a column of collected checkers, placing the jumped piece on the bottom of your stack.

4 If a Soldier collects checkers, he can still only move like a Soldier—in one direction. If an Officer collects checkers, he can move in any direction.

5 It gets even better. If a column gets jumped, just the top checker is taken. This will leave another checker—maybe an Officer, maybe a Soldier—in place at the top of the stack. The stack moves according to that top checker.

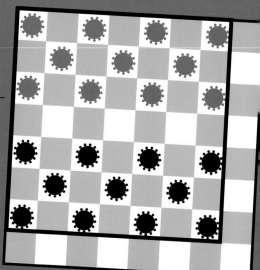

6 Play according to the color of the top checker, too. So if a black checker was removed and a red was underneath, red now controls the stack.

The Goal Play the game until all your opponent's playing pieces have been captured or until you have cornered him and he cannot move.

And the winner is! Whoever blocks so well that the opponent cannot move. Or whoever captures all the opponent's pieces.

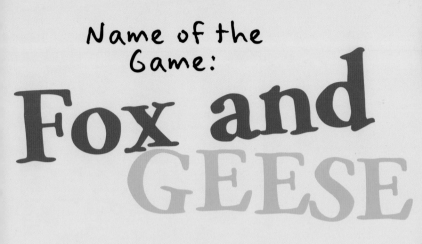

Name of the Game:

Fox and GEESE

Man, are there ever a lot of games with animals in the title!
And there's always the player who gets just one checker. Just like in this game of Fox and Geese.

One player gets 17 pieces to be the Geese; the other player gets 1 piece to be the Fox.

The game board is in the shape of a cross. See the diagram on page 48. You might want to sketch in the lines on the board for this game. The Geese fill in the first three lines and then the first and last squares of the next two lines. The Fox takes position on the fourth square of the fifth line. He should have a Goose three squares away on both sides.

Flip a coin to see who plays the Fox. Geese start the game with the first move.

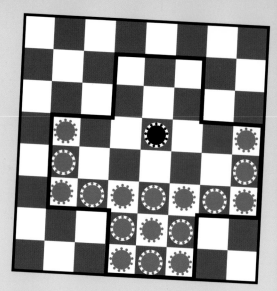

Your Move

 1 The Fox can move in any direction. I mean any direction: forward, backward, on the diagonal, even to the side.

2 He moves just one space at a time.

 3 The Fox wants to jump as many Geese as possible. He may only jump, though, if he can land on an empty sp

4 The Fox must work around the board, jumping Geese and moving them off to the side. Multiple jumps are allowed.

5 The Geese can move forward and to the side only. And only one move at a time. All their efforts will be to corner the Fox.

The Goal The Geese want to trap the Fox so he can no longer move. The Fox wants to jump over all the Geese.

And the winner is! The player who accomplishes his goal.

Name of the Game:

Wildebeest

This game is played on a board with a cross-shaped playing field. The same as in the game of Fox and Geese.

Each player gets 11 pieces.

You place your checkers on the game board one at a time. See diagram on page 52. BUT—and this is important—you can't have any of your own checkers side by side in any line during setup. Neither can your opponent. There must be space between the checker pieces. This means you cannot play all the checkers at the same time.

Flip a coin or guess a number to see who goes first.

Your Move

Taking turns, move a piece either vertically or horizontally.

Try to get 3 of your own pieces to line up. You can add checkers as space opens up on the board.

3

When you place a new checker on the board, make sure that it is not adjacent to any of your other pieces. You'll want to maneuver these new guys into place, just like you did with the other pieces. At the same time, try to block your opponent from getting 3 in a row.

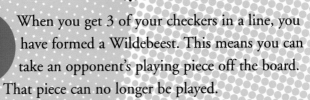 When you get 3 of your checkers in a line, you have formed a Wildebeest. This means you can take an opponent's playing piece off the board. That piece can no longer be played.

5 Then you keep playing.

The Goal Line up your checkers before your opponent does.

And the winner is! Whoever removes the most of his opponent's playing pieces from the board is the winner.

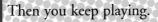

Name of the Game:
Horseshoe

This is a quick game. And it's easy to learn.

Each player gets 2 checkers, one color for each person.

Place checkers in the four corners of the game board.

Decide who starts the game.

Your Move

1 You can only use the five spots indicated on the diagram. You might want to sketch in the lines on the board for this game. The first player moves in the only place he can—to the center square.

2 By turns, each player moves from place to place, following the lines on the game board.

3 When one person traps the other so he cannot move, the game is over.

The Goal The goal is to block your opponent so he cannot move.

And the winner is! Whoever keeps the opponent from moving wins the game.

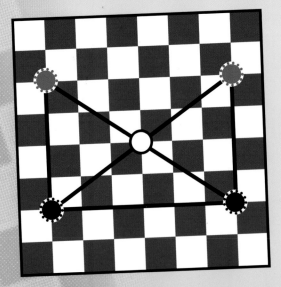

AND THEN THERE Was One

Here are a few games you can play all by your lonesome. These are for those times when you just need to be alone. Many of these games are puzzles and once you figure them out, the game is over. (And if you get to feeling like you don't have a friend in the world, invite somebody over to play one of the two-player games in this book.)

Name of the Game:
Catching the Pigs

Children love to chase pigs around the farm (or the apartment!).

You get 4 pieces—2 red and 2 black.

Place the checkers on the fourth row up from the bottom of the board, as shown in the diagram. Start by putting a black checker on a black square, skip a box, and now put a red checker down (it will also be on a black square). Staying in this same line, go to the opposite side of the board. Put a black checker on a white square. Skip a square and place a red checker on a white square. See the diagram for how the board should look. The red checkers are the Kids; the black checkers are the big, fat Pigs.

Both Kids checkers must move first.

oink

oink

Oink

Oink

56

Your Move

1 Start by moving both Kids checkers at the same time. They can go forward, backward, or sideways.

2 Now you move the Pigs—both of them—one space each. The checkers can move forward, backward, or sideways.

3 The Pigs try to stay out of the way of the Kids, and the Kids try to catch the Pigs by landing on the same space with one of them.

4 You move both Kids checkers at the same time (but not necessarily in the same direction) and both Pigs checkers at the same time (but not necessarily in the same direction). Only move one space at a time. Remember: You don't move on the diagonal in this game.

The Goal
Catch those Pigs! And keep away from those Kids!

And the winner is! The Kid checker needs to work its way toward the Pig checker, until they share the same space. Once you've figured out how to play this game, challenge someone to play the Kids checkers and you play the Pigs checkers.

Name of the Game:

Hey!
GET OUTTA MY LINE

This is one of those games where the checker pieces are not allowed to be in the same line as another checker. They are loners, the whole lot.

Choose any 8 pieces. It doesn't matter the color. Use both if you'd like.

There is no setup for this game. You'll be placing pieces on the board one at a time.

Look over all the little checkers you have. Which one looks like he's been the best today? Choose that one to start the game.

Your Move There are sixty-four squares on the board. You can use any you want. Starting with your favorite checker, put all 8 checkers on the board.

The Goal Here's the catch. Remember these guys are loners? They want to be in a line all by themselves. So look the board over and make sure that you've set up these pieces so there is no other checker in line with another. Not horizontally. Not diagonally. Not even vertically. Man, the game just got hard!

And the winner is!

Well, I hope you are, 'cause you're playing all by yourself.

See the solution on page 64.

Name of the Game:

Leapfrog

This is another one of those games you can play by yourself. It's fun!

You need 16 checkers to play this game. Use 15 red pieces and just 1 black piece. I know he might look lonely, but that old checker will be there at the end.

The black checker goes into the bottom left-hand corner, and then the red fill in all the spaces until the bottom two rows you are playing on are full. See diagram.

It doesn't matter which checker you begin with, he just needs to be able to jump over someone.

Your Move

 The pieces can move forward, backward, and even sideways, jumping each other.

No diagonal jumping.

 No moving out of those three rows of the checkerboard.

4 Jump in such a way that the black checker makes the final move and remains alone on the board.

The Goal Your goal is to jump all the red checkers—every last one of them—and remove them from the board.

And the winner is!
That last little black checker! That's the one who should make the final jump.

Name of the Game:

Solitaire Pyramid Checkers

**Once you learn this game, challenge
your friends to see if they can do it.**

Your Move

1 You get 10 checkers. Starting on the fourth line from the bottom of the checkerboard, place 4 checkers on the black squares. On the fifth line, on the second black square from the left, place your next 3 checkers. See the pattern?

2 The third line up will get 2 checkers. You'll start on the second black square.

 3 The top line gets just 1 checker piece. The third black square from the left is the home for that final checker. See the diagram to check your setup.

4 Now choose just 3 checkers to move to create a new pyramid. Which pieces do you move? Did it work? That's part of the game.

The Goal Moving just 3 checkers, turn the pyramid upside down.

And the winner is!
Well, you are!

See the solution on page 64.

Solitaire
Pyramid
Checkers
Solution